STÉPHANE COMPOINT

BURIED TREASURES

Uncovering Secrets of the Past

Abrams Books for Young Readers
New York

Library of Congress Cataloging-in-Publication Data

Compoint, Stéphane.
  Buried treasures / Stéphane Compoint.
    p. cm.
  ISBN 978-0-8109-9781-3 (alk. paper)
  1. Antiquities—Juvenile literature. 2. Archaeology—History—Juvenile literature. 3. Civilization, Ancient—Juvenile literature. I. Title.
  CC171.C655 2011
  930.1—dc22
                              2010021626

Originally published in French by Éditions de la Martinière
English translation copyright © 2011 Harry N. Abrams, Inc.
English translation by Graham Robert Edwards
Photographs by Stéphane Compoint
Art direction by Benoit Nacci
Book design by Valerie Roland

Printed and bound in China
10 9 8 7 6 5 4 3 2 1

Abrams Books for Young Readers are available at special discounts when purchased in quantity for premiums and promotions as well as fundraising or educational use. Special editions can also be created to specification. For details, contact specialmarkets@abramsbooks.com or the address below.

THE ART OF BOOKS SINCE 1949
115 West 18th Street
New York, NY 10011
www.abramsbooks.com

Contents

Introduction

I've loved photography ever since I was a child. At eighteen I became a press photographer. At that age, most of your life lies ahead of you. But you still need to be careful about the choices you make. It's all too easy to get stuck. Even now, photography is all I know. Fortunately I enjoy it as much as I ever did.

One reason the work of archaeologists across the world interests me so much as a photographer is the variety. You'll see that in this book—there are lots of locations pictured—and it's true that I'm an inquisitive traveler. A second, more important reason is the impressive skill archaeologists have of combining cultural knowledge with scientific expertise. On more than one occasion, having traveled to the middle of nowhere, I have felt as if I were listening to a top-class lecture at an academic institution. The archaeologists I've met have all had the detective skills and determination of Sherlock Holmes, even though it may take years for them to have anything to show for it. The men and women whose work I describe in this book are something of a cross

between a scientist and Indiana Jones. Sometimes they dig away for thirty years before their hunches and determination yield a lost treasure.

Traces of the great Lighthouse of Alexandria, mummies two thousand years old, the bones of a Baluchitherium (the largest land mammal yet known), and the Nazca Lines traced out in the Peruvian Andean desert—these are some of the sites pictured in this book. The whole world recognizes their uniqueness, and they bear witness to the richness of cultures that came before ours. Today's scientific archaeologists have the good fortune of working at a time when technology can help them find worlds that till now were completely buried. We live in a time when the pace of life is ever quickening. But it seems to me that the better humankind understands its past, the better it will envision its future.

Such, then, is the quest of this book.
So please, follow me!

STÉPHANE COMPOINT

Archaeological Missions Around the World

**THE NORTH POLE:
A TREASURE ADRIFT**
ARCTIC OCEAN

THE MYTHIC BLUE BEAR
ALASKA

**THE CELTS:
CIVILIZED BARBARIANS**
FRANCE AND ITALY

**POMPEII:
A CITY PRESERVED**
ITALY

ATLANTIC OCEAN

**ALEXANDRIA:
A DROWNED WONDER**
EGYPT

PACIFIC OCEAN

**ABEL: WORLD'S
FIRST HUMAN?**
CHADIAN DESERT

**CAHUACHI: AN
OPEN-AIR MUSEUM**
PERU

**EASTER ISLAND:
A LOST CIVILIZATION**
CHILE

THE ORIGINAL
OLYMPIC GAMES
GREECE

ZEUGMA: A SUNKEN CITY
ZEUGMA, TURKEY

THE DINOSAURS OF MONGOLIA
GOBI DESERT, MONGOLIA

USERKARE:
THE MISSING PHARAOH
VALLEY OF THE NILE, EGYPT

THE BALUCHITHERIUM
BALUCHISTAN, PAKISTAN

MUMMIES DEEP
IN THE DESERT
KHARGA OASIS, EGYPT

PACIFIC OCEAN

INDIAN OCEAN

Alexandria: A Drowned Wonder

Who could have guessed that four thousand years separated this man and this stone statue? Founded about twenty-three centuries ago by Alexander the Great, Alexandria, with its million inhabitants, was second only to Rome in the ancient world. Its library and museum were among the earliest in history, and it was famous both for its revolutionary urban planning and for the great lighthouse that was one of the Seven Wonders of the Ancient World. Built on the tiny offshore island of Pharos, the lighthouse was around 390 to 450 feet high. Its fires were a guide to sailors for more than a thousand years. It was damaged and eventually reduced to ruins by a series of violent earthquakes.

In 1994, a team of French scientists, led by the archaeologist Jean-Yves Empereur, discovered more than two thousand blocks of ancient stonework, including sphinxes, obelisks, and royal statues, revealing the splendor of a lost civilization.

Among the remains on the sea floor, many items have been hoisted to the surface for restoration and exhibition in museums. The sphinx in this picture, a creature with a human head and the body of a lion, was discovered intact twenty-five feet underwater.

▶ **After several months' work,** there was intense emotion as the huge statue of King Ptolemy II, who built much of Alexandria, was raised to the surface. A great deal of care was necessary because the statue had been underwater for fifteen centuries. With its crown, head, and legs, the statue was nearly forty feet tall and was located at the lighthouse entrance.

Found! One of the Seven Wonders of the Ancient World.

▲ **The head of Ptolemy II's statue** was found some distance away from the torso. Every piece of the statue was datable from the inscriptions on the stonework.

▲ **In order to identify the statue as quickly as possible, the archaeological divers** took measurements of the colossal torso. It was fifteen feet long and weighed around thirteen tons.

▼ **Ptolemy II's statue** is conveyed amid the taxis and traffic jams of the city he built long ago. It took six months to clear the statue of salt and other minerals before it could be exhibited to the world.

◄ **Once recovered from the water and restored,** the various parts of Ptolemy II's statue could be reassembled.

▼ **In order to raise** Ptolemy II's statue, the divers put chains around the stonework and fitted it with underwater balloons to lift and turn it.

15

▼ **Though he does not realize it,** six-year-old Balah is playing in the middle of a labyrinthine cemetery from ancient times. His knowledge of the place helped the archaeologists draw up an early plan of the necropolis in record time. Speed was important in a race against highway bulldozers.

While excavating for the Alexandria-to-Cairo highway, the largest necropolis in antiquity—Shatby—was found, comprising several thousand tombs.

▶ **This coffin and sarcophagus belonged to a noble family.** The paintings, protected from light and air for two thousand years, still maintain their brilliant colors. This archaeologist is using tracing paper to make a rubbing of the coffin's patterns.

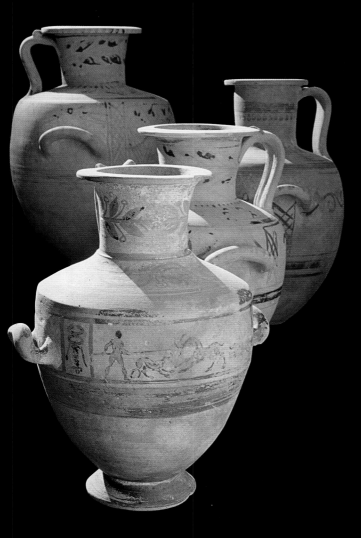

Vases, statuettes, vials, and oil lamps have been discovered in abundance. They date from the Ptolemaic period (323 BCE–30 CE) and accompanied the dead in their final resting place.

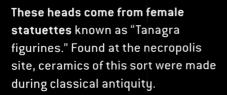

These heads come from female statuettes known as "Tanagra figurines." Found at the necropolis site, ceramics of this sort were made during classical antiquity.

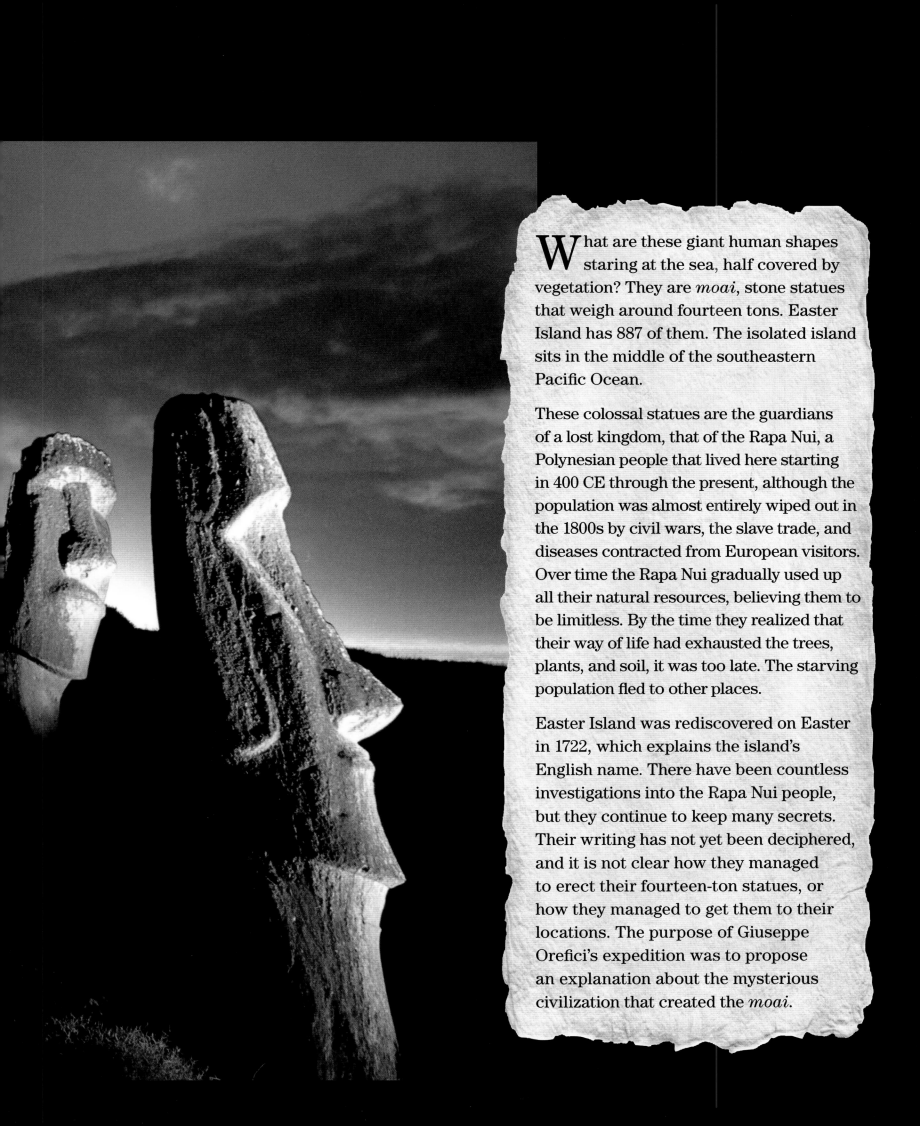

What are these giant human shapes staring at the sea, half covered by vegetation? They are *moai*, stone statues that weigh around fourteen tons. Easter Island has 887 of them. The isolated island sits in the middle of the southeastern Pacific Ocean.

These colossal statues are the guardians of a lost kingdom, that of the Rapa Nui, a Polynesian people that lived here starting in 400 CE through the present, although the population was almost entirely wiped out in the 1800s by civil wars, the slave trade, and diseases contracted from European visitors. Over time the Rapa Nui gradually used up all their natural resources, believing them to be limitless. By the time they realized that their way of life had exhausted the trees, plants, and soil, it was too late. The starving population fled to other places.

Easter Island was rediscovered on Easter in 1722, which explains the island's English name. There have been countless investigations into the Rapa Nui people, but they continue to keep many secrets. Their writing has not yet been deciphered, and it is not clear how they managed to erect their fourteen-ton statues, or how they managed to get them to their locations. The purpose of Giuseppe Orefici's expedition was to propose an explanation about the mysterious civilization that created the *moai*.

The Rapa Nui, a civilization that was isolated from the rest of the world for twelve hundred years.

◀ **Like all the kavakava *moai*,** this one was buried in front of its owner's house and represented his soul. It was carved from the wood of the toromiro tree, which has become extinct in the wild. Only the tribe's big chiefs were entitled to a stone *moai*.

◀ **On the slopes of the extinct volcano Rano Raraku,** Giuseppe Orefici's team investigates a group of fallen *moai* dating from the sixteenth century. The archaeologists measure the size of their hands, chests, and faces. These dimensions reflect the style and time period during which the statues were carved.

▼ **The largest—but unfinished—***moai* is known as El Gigante and weighs approximately 150 tons and is 72 feet tall. Had it been finished, it may have looked like this *moai*. We are not sure why the Rapa Nui continued to carve such large statues, though rivalry between tribes could have been one reason.

▲ **Remains of villages** and numerous caves on this volcanic island contain petroglyphs, or rock engravings. Those above represent the god of fertility (Makemake). On the left, Giuseppe Orefici examines petroglyphs of large fish, which symbolized abundance, or else of birds, which symbolized freedom.

Femme de l'Isle de Pâque.

Homme de l'Isle de Pâques.

▲ **The *moai* of Ahu Naunau** at Anakena are close to the island's northern shoreline. These figures are placed parallel to the line of the rising and setting of the sun. Their distinguishing feature is their *pukao*, or headpieces. Made of red volcanic rock, they may represent hair tied in a topknot.

▲ **When the island was discovered** by Europeans in 1774, Pascuan civilization, depicted in these period engravings, had already been weakened by the exhaustion of local natural resources. Infections introduced by the explorers proved deadly—the native population had no immunity against European bacteria and viruses.

▶ **During the eighteenth and nineteenth centuries,** the island's 1,200 *moai* were cast down by the population when the shortage of natural resources provoked a revolution. Researchers are attempting to pinpoint the causes of these dramatic events through soil analysis, using advanced techniques such as microscopic electronic scanning.

▼ **This stick engraved in Rongorongo script** is more than six feet long. No one has yet succeeded in deciphering its hieroglyphs.

▲ **Unlike the *moai* of the island's leaders,** these kavakava figures were carved out of toromiro wood, regarded as a precious material. They were buried under the doorways of Rapa Nui, which accounts for their excellent state of preservation.

▶ **These fish hooks date from the fifth century CE.** They are not unlike others of similar date found two thousand miles away on the Marquesas Islands. It has been concluded that Polynesians used the limited means of sea travel available at the time to reach what was then an uninhabited island. But no one can determine exactly when that occurred; some researchers think it may have been as late as 1200 CE.

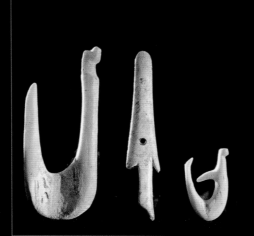

In southern Egypt, in the middle of the desert, the Kharga Oasis has been an important staging post for travelers west of the Nile for thousands of years. When examining the cliff edges around the oasis, four scientists undertaking excavations in the area happened upon groups of tombs (necropolises) in the cliffside, where they found several hundred bodies, all mummified.

Though death claimed them more than two thousand years ago, these bodies have been well preserved by the extremely dry atmosphere of the desert. It is sometimes assumed that mummification was only for the powerful, such as pharaohs. Although in the time of the pharaohs the technique of embalming was for only the elite, it became simpler as time went on and was gradually extended to everyone. These remains show that the same funeral procedure was eventually available to peasants, soldiers, workers, and their children.

Researchers created a field laboratory and used modern techniques (such as X-rays) to discover the diet, daily life, state of health, and cause of death of these ancient Egyptians. Here, the French historian Françoise Dunand numbers and records the location of these mummies before removing them from their tombs. After they are examined, each one will be restored to its original position.

▲ **Weighing on average only a little more than twenty-six pounds**—because once dehydrated, a human body loses four-fifths of its weight—the mummies are easily removed from their tombs and taken to the laboratory, where they will receive a thorough medical examination.

◀ **Each necropolis contains** several mummies laid out on the sand inside the hollows of the desert cliffs. Some of them, embalmed according to the rites of ancient Egypt, were still covered in the bands in which they had originally been wrapped. Scientific analysis has shown that each tomb, placed against the cave wall, was occupied by members of the same family.

The faces of these mummies wear expressions of peace and repose.

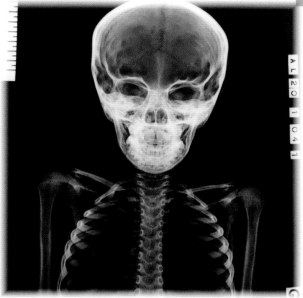

▶ **X-ray photos in the laboratory** shed light on the lifestyle of this little-understood population. They revealed, for instance, numerous wounds caused by agricultural labor and a great number of diseases. It was therefore reasonable to conclude that this was a population of peasants and manual laborers.

▲ **Minute examination of the skulls and bodies** of these mummies held some surprises for French anthropologist Jean-Louis Heim. He discovered that the average adult was much taller than Europeans were prior to the early nineteenth century. One of them, indeed, was six feet tall.

▼ **Even after two thousand years,** the facial expressions and henna-colored hair and eyelids were still intact and gave the corpses something of a personal character. This was all due to the mummification process. It is not surprising, then, that the scientific investigators gave them names rather than numbers.

Across southern Peru and northern Chile, between the Pacific Ocean and the Andes mountain range, is a land totally devoid of rainfall. Seen from an aircraft, the desert reveals huge drawings in the rock (geoglyphs) several miles in length. Between 400 and 650 CE, the Nazca people created them with startling precision. Some are very well preserved. Human, animal, and geometrical forms constitute an amazing open-air art gallery that can be seen only from above.

The tenth-century "Atacama Giant" (pictured) is the biggest human-shaped representation in the world, being nearly three hundred feet from top to toe. It depicts a deified chieftain, with bird-of-prey feathers on top of its head and cat whiskers on either side; both creatures were regarded as gods by the peoples of pre-Columbian America.

But how did the Nazca people trace them out? What do they mean? The discovery in 1997 of Cahuachi, the Nazca people's ceremonial center, by an archaeological team led by Giuseppe Orefici, was a step forward in understanding their culture—a culture that left behind no written record. On the other hand, the Nazca left pyramids, necropolises, mummies, cloth, and pottery of exceptional quality together with complex networks of irrigation.

◄ **This two-thousand-year-old geoglyph,** measuring 319 feet by 213 feet, represents a hummingbird, one of the main Nazca divinities. In the desert, only the top layer, comprising iron-rich pebbles, is of a dark color. As soon as you dig down, the ground is an off-white color. The Nazca used this feature to trace out all kinds of shapes.

Impossible to see from the ground, the enormous geoglyphs of the Nazca are visible only from the air.

▼ **The nine-fingered monkey** on the left, measuring 305 feet by 190 feet, and the 101-foot killer whale on the right were drawn at the same period. Such designs indicate that the Nazca wished to please these animals, whose divine power they feared.

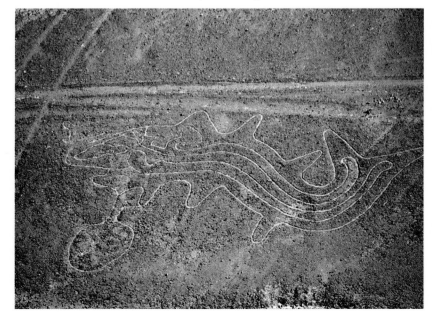

▶ **These cloth materials,** discovered during excavation, are of astonishingly high quality. The coat (top left) is stitched with hundreds of male figures just over an inch tall, all different and three-dimensional. Represented is a procession of musicians and dancers following the line of a geoglyph. On the edge of the coat (bottom left) are hummingbirds, slightly under an inch in size, seeking nectar from flowers.

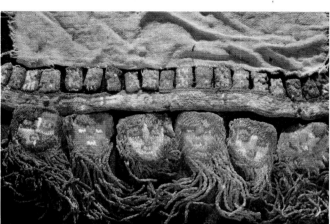

◀ **Painted pots are decorated** with all sort of divinities, including man-cats, man-birds, and man-serpents.

▼ **At Cahuachi, archaeologists have found** hundreds of early panpipes, known as *antara*. They are ceramic and make a unique sound. Human heads, sacrificed to the gods, have also been found here with hair perfectly preserved by the dry atmospheric conditions. The attached rope was used either to transport the skull or to wear it on a belt.

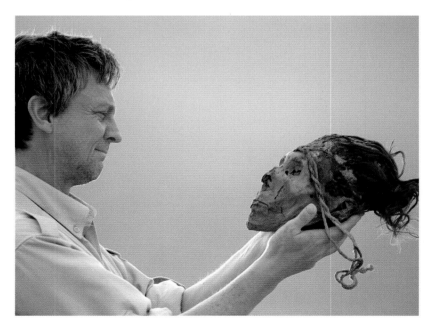

What animal holds the all-time record for size and weight? If you thought you might be able to see it in a zoo, you'd be disappointed, because it died out millions of years ago. For centuries the Mongol nomads of the Gobi Desert dug up the bones of huge, strange animals, which they called dragons because of their large size and odd shapes. Reassembling the skeletons, researchers realized that they were fossilized dinosaurs, animals that dominated the earth until they disappeared 65 million years ago.

The vegetation of their day, which was like that of today's African savannah, also died and turned into desert. And most of the animal chain, including dinosaurs, that depended upon the vegetation died out with it. Today, the Gobi Desert is one of the largest and most hostile deserts in the world.

In a number of excavations, around sixty species of dinosaurs have been discovered there, many of which were found by Roy Chapman Andrews, a researcher and adventurer, whose life is rumored to have inspired the movie character Indiana Jones. His fabulous haul of dinosaur bones has been shown in numerous exhibitions worldwide. With its fifty-ton weight, the animal pictured here would have weighed as much as ten elephants.

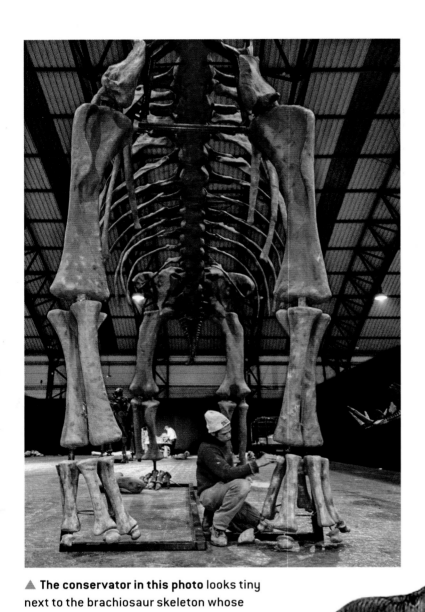

▲ **The conservator in this photo** looks tiny next to the brachiosaur skeleton whose foot he is working on. The anatomy of this skeleton differs little from today's animals, a fact that made it easier to assemble this one. The bones here probably belonged to several different individual dinosaurs.

For dinosaur hunters, the Gobi Desert contains rich pickings.

◀ **It is thought that the skin of dinosaurs** was similar to that of today's lizards, as this reconstruction shows. To have enough energy and to develop such an enormous body, the brachiosaur must have eaten around a ton and a half of branches, leaves, and grass every day. Using its very long neck (twelve vertebrae, each one almost two and a half feet wide), it had a reach equal to approximately four floors of a typical modern building.

▲ **The brachiosaur had a thickset head** with a wide snout. But compared to its body, its head was rather small. The teeth in its jaws were like stakes, and it had nostrils on the top of its head, a feature that explains why, for a long time, people thought it lived underwater.

▶ **In spite of its great height** (forty feet), this young diplodocus probably belonged to a herd of twenty to thirty others; they sought safety in numbers to escape predators like the infamous T. rex.

Life-size reconstructions make it possible to visualize the animals that roamed the earth 65 million years ago.

▶ **Because it was too heavy and ungainly to run,** stegosaur used its tail for self-defense. This tail had four sharp spines, each of which could be more than three feet long. The bony plates on its back helped regulate its body temperature, acting like solar panels.

Bit by bit we can see a face looking at us out of the mosaic: a brilliantly assembled portrait, certain lines of which suggest Alexander the Great. Without him, the ancient city of Zeugma would probably never have existed. On the borders of modern-day Turkey and Syria, Zeugma was especially rich in mosaics. "Zeugma" means "bridge" or "link" in ancient Greek, and the city was situated on the shores of the Euphrates, on the silk route, which made it prosperous. Archaeologists were aware that there was an ancient city here, but had never been able to explore it.

Turkey's decision to build a dam, or barrage, on the river in 1995 prompted the foundation of an emergency archaeological mission made up of French, Turks, and Americans. They had only nine months to attempt to rescue whatever could be salvaged before the valley disappeared underwater. They discovered houses, wells, drains, statues, furniture, paintings, and fourteen mosaics that came from a luxurious Roman villa—Zeugma, at the time, had been inhabited by Romans.

Once the excavations were over, what had been saved from the water was enough to reveal that Zeugma was a frontier city, midway between the Greco-Roman world and the Orient.

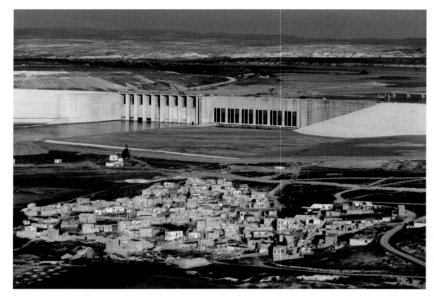 

▲ **Located a third of a mile upstream of the ancient site of Zeugma,** the village of Belkis in October 1999 (left) and in June 2000 (right). In the background is the Birecik barrage. In less than a year, the ancient city was drowned, and with it thirty or so outstanding mosaics, paintings, coins, and other valuable objects.

A race to save Zeugma's treasures from the waters of the Birecik barrage.

▲ **In order to remove the Roman villa's fourteen mosaics,** specialist archaeologists worked for thousands of hours on an area about six hundred square yards. The work was done in several stages. After careful cleaning and stabilization of the most fragile portions, the mosaics were glued to thick cotton material and cut into panels, with special care taken not to cut across figurative areas. To prevent breakage, the largest mosaics were rolled onto large-diameter cylinders. Despite the archaeologists' best efforts, many other mosaics could not be salvaged because there wasn't enough time.

◄ **This mosaic is one of the major discoveries at Zeugma.** It refers to the myth of Queen Pasiphaë (seated extreme left), the wife of King Minos of Crete. The god Poseidon caused her to fall in love with a bull, and she hid in a wooden cow (being made by Daedalus and Icarus on the right) in order to seduce him. Their union produced the Minotaur, which had a man's body and the head of a bull. In the top right of the picture is the palace of the labyrinth that Ariadne (second from left) helped Theseus escape from using the thread she gave him.

▶ **This five-foot-high bronze statue** of Ares (Mars) is one of six known bronze representations of the god of war. It is the only sculpture discovered on this site.

The Mythic Blue Bear

Lynn Schooler lives in Juneau, Alaska's capital, where he has been a guide for more than twenty years. His work includes escorting filmmakers, wildlife photographers, and adventurers to the wild landscape of the Arctic, with its fjords, forests, and glaciers.

In 1990, Michio Hoshino, a famous Japanese photographer working for *National Geographic*, asked Lynn to take him somewhere to see an extremely shy animal: the glacier bear, also called a blue bear. Named because of its fur—which has silvery glints—blue bears are notoriously hard to find. It is thought that there are now only about a hundred of them left, scattered over a territory two and a half times the area of Texas and very sparsely populated, with only about six hundred thousand inhabitants. For more than ten years the two tried to track down and photograph this cousin to the brown bear. They were never successful in their quest, but the photographer and his guide became firm friends.

Then, years later, Lynn Schooler had a brief encounter with this creature of myths and stories when he least expected it.

▲ **Adaptability, good judgment, and respect for the environment** are needed to be a guide. In the undisturbed forest that borders Frederick Sound, about sixty miles south of Juneau, Lynn Schooler looks for traces and clues to the presence of blue bears along the riverbank.

▲ **The territory and food sources of the blue bear,** like those of its cousin, the brown bear, are varied, a fact that does not make looking for it any easier. Here, Lynn Schooler is seen exploring Glacier Bay National Park, thirty miles north of Juneau.

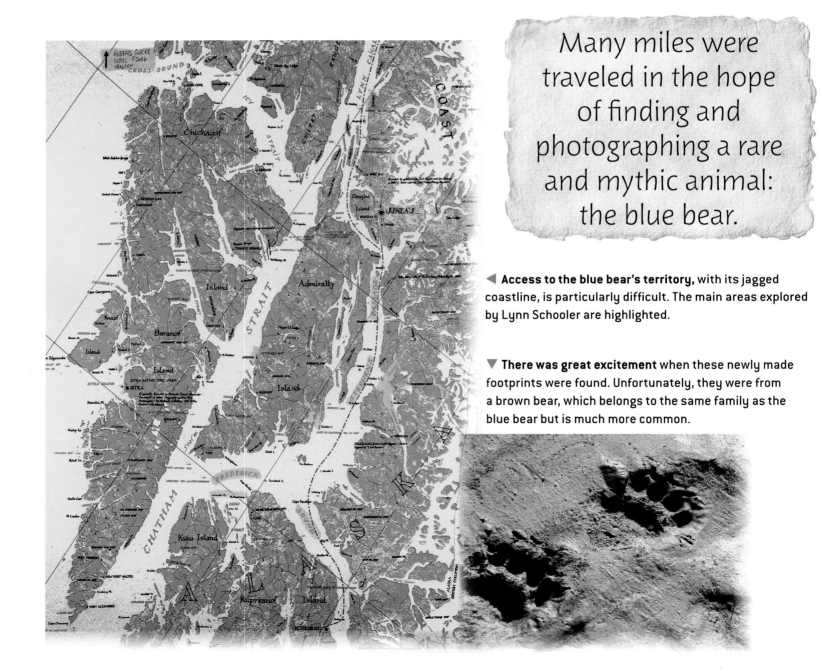

Many miles were traveled in the hope of finding and photographing a rare and mythic animal: the blue bear.

◀ **Access to the blue bear's territory,** with its jagged coastline, is particularly difficult. The main areas explored by Lynn Schooler are highlighted.

▼ **There was great excitement** when these newly made footprints were found. Unfortunately, they were from a brown bear, which belongs to the same family as the blue bear but is much more common.

◄ **Lynn Schooler travels upstream along a river,** where glaciers hang over the watercourse. It's a risky journey because huge ice blocks can break off at any moment. When exploring the fjords, guides use boats that are also their main residences when they're anchored in the Juneau harbor.

▼ **An extremely rare shot of a blue bear,** taken by the famous wildlife photographer John Hyde.

The Celts: Civilized Barbarians

People in mainland Europe and America often assume that Celtic remains are found only in the British Isles. It came as something of a surprise to archaeologists, then, when excavations in France and Italy between 2002 and 2007, prior to the building of an east–west European high-speed rail link, uncovered evidence of settlement by the people of bards and druids. Since then, it has become clearer that the remains of a poorly understood civilization, the Celts, actually comprised a mosaic of peoples extending from southern Britain to northern Spain and from Brittany to Hungary.

The gold, bronze, and ceramic goods discovered in excavations reveal the civilized nature of this people, which is often portrayed in school or at the cinema as barbaric. The three thousand menhirs of the lines discovered at Carnac in Brittany (pictured) could only have been arranged by an advanced and ingenious civilization, one capable of placing stones, each weighing several tons, in perfectly straight lines. Who were these people responsible for placing these standing stones? Why did they erect them? There are lots of unanswered questions, but it is certain that the Celts were there and remained for centuries.

◄ **An industrial vacuum cleaner** was used to clear these Celtic burial places of the earth that covered them. Such tombs, found simultaneously in Champagne (left) and in Italy (below), contained jewelry and complete warrior kits (sword, scabbard, spear, and javelin).

▲ **The Champagne region,** in eastern France, is one of the areas affected by the route of the Paris–Strasbourg high-speed rail link. Before any rails were laid, the topsoil was removed using a mechanical shovel at ten-meter intervals (slightly under thirty-three feet) over a distance of 186 miles. Archaeologists and scientists were then able to examine these breaches in the ground for two years—known as "preventive archaeology."

▼ **Discovered in excavations near Bologna** in northern Italy, this collection of dishes, vases, and vials was intact, having been simply a funerary deposit. They share Celtic and Etruscan features, which is further proof that the two civilizations long cohabited in this region.

Before the Romans conquered Europe, the Celts occupied a huge territory. Gradually, more traces of them are coming to light.

▼ **This collection of weaponry** shows that the Celts were even better than the Greeks and Romans at making swords, scabbards, spears, and helmets. This skill, which explains their expansion, was so outstanding that even today's smiths find it challenging to make objects of similar quality.

▼ **Discovered during excavations** in the south of France, this bronze helmet, gold-plated and encrusted with coral, is a masterpiece of Celtic precious metalwork. To this day, no one is able to say for whom it was intended.

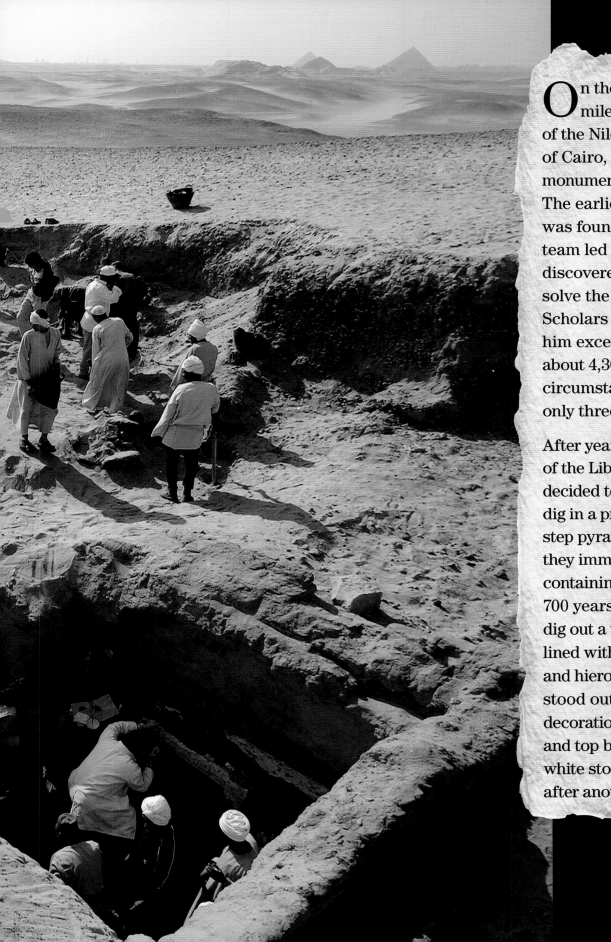

On the edge of the Sahara, a few miles west of the palm plantations of the Nile Valley and fifteen miles south of Cairo, is the world's oldest stone monument, the step pyramid at Saqqara. The earliest capital of Egypt, Memphis, was founded here. Here, too, in 2002, a team led by Egyptologist Vassil Dobrev discovered a necropolis that may well solve the mystery of Pharaoh Userkare. Scholars know practically nothing about him except that he came to the throne about 4,300 years ago in mysterious circumstances and that his reign lasted only three or four years.

After years of research in the archives of the Library of Cairo, Vassil Dobrev decided to engage local workmen to help dig in a precise place, 330 yards from the step pyramid. Just over three feet down they immediately came across sarcophagi containing mummies dating from around 700 years BCE. As they continued to dig out a trench, they discovered a road lined with tombs bearing inscriptions and hieroglyphs. One tomb in particular stood out because of its quality and decoration. Digging exposed the uprights and top beam, which were composed of white stone. They then had one surprise after another.

◀ **Less than two feet under the sand,** archaeologists came across a sarcophagus in perfect condition dating from 700 BCE. Once it was placed under the tent and opened, they found an intact mummy, which they set out to examine and identify.

◀ **Among the remains of the funerary temple,** six scholars move a well-secured sarcophagus that weighs 330 pounds. They are moving it to a building where the mummies can be examined and restored prior to provisional storage in the museum's basement.

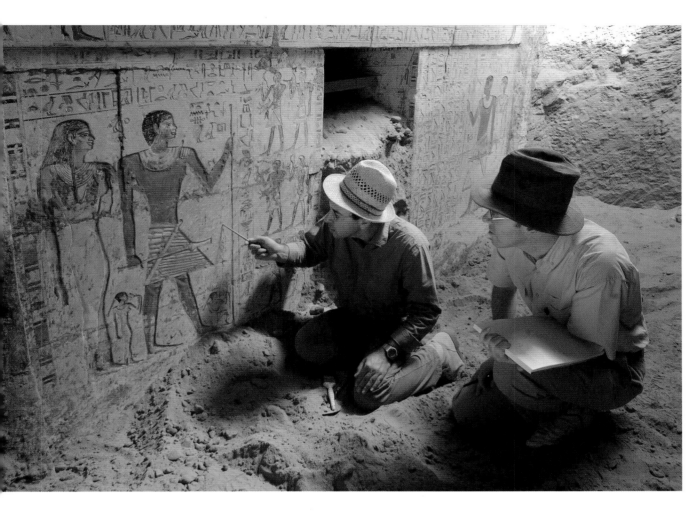

◀ **The grains of sand have barely been brushed away** before the superb multicolored facade of the tomb offers its early secrets. Once they have deciphered the hieroglyphs, Vassil Dobrev and his team realize that they have found the family cave of Pharaoh Userkare's high priest. They're getting warm.

Several feet below the sand, remains from as long as 4,300 years ago appear before the eyes of archaeologists.

▼ **In this historical reconstruction,** artists are decorating the tomb of Userkare's high priest. The natural pigments used to color the hieroglyphs and the persons illustrated were of such high quality that they have not faded. Forty-three centuries later, they still have the same vivid colors.

▶ **The most important event in a pharaoh's reign** was the building of his pyramid, the tomb in which he would be laid after his death. It was thought to be the only means whereby he could obtain eternal life. This historical reconstruction, which was used to illustrate a film about Pharaoh Userkare, shows the king in the company of his queen and court. He is visiting his chief architect before fixing on the exact site of his future pyramid.

What on earth can this man be looking for, kneeling down, scratching at the sandy ground in the vastness of the desert in Chad? He is the French paleontologist Michel Brunet, and he is at the point of finding remains that prove that humankind's earliest individuals were born here, in the heart of the Sahara.

For over a century, paleontologists worldwide had searched for humanity's origins. In 1974, investigators found a skeleton 3.2 million years old in Ethiopia, which they named "Lucy"; she was believed to be humanity's most senior ancestor. The world's scientific community was convinced that the earliest members of the human race originated on the high plateaus of eastern Africa, in Ethiopia. It was there that the oldest specimens in the world so far had been found. They thought Brunet was crazy.

Yet his determination eventually paid off. In January 1995, he and his small scientific team of five found the jaw of an Australopithecus 3.5 million years old. He nicknamed the find "Abel." Six years later, he found a skull and several teeth nearly 7 million years old, which he named "Toumaï" (meaning "hope of life" in the local language). These two discoveries revolutionized ideas about the origins of mankind.

▼ **After sifting through tons of sand,** researchers come across the fossilized teeth of animals that lived in the period of Australopithecus. Many miles of desert have been picked through with a fine-tooth comb.

▲ **Fossils found around Abel's jaw** dated back 3.5 million years. Here, Michel Brunet comes across a fossilized catfish. Today, this site is a desert, but it once had trees that lined Lake Chad, which was then an enormous inland sea.

▲ **The fossils here are displayed** in a lecture room at the University of Poitiers in France. At the time the photo was taken, Michel Brunet was a professor there.

◀ **Shown here are earlier species** of the crocodile, gazelle, horse, and elephant. Some four thousand fossils of animals and plants were discovered in the same geological strata as Abel and Toumaï. They enabled scientists to date these australopithecines more accurately.

In the Sahara, paleontologists find bones that offer valuable information about the dawn of humanity.

◀ **Michel Brunet holds Abel's tiny jawbone.** His discovery of Abel in West Africa rewrote the history of the earliest hominids. On the left is a three-dimensional clay reconstruction of Abel's face, informed by Brunet's discoveries.

Pompeii: A City Preserved

The violent eruption of Vesuvius in 79 CE wiped the prosperous Roman imperial city of Pompeii off the map. The site lay forgotten for eighteen centuries.

Yet for the historians and archaeologists who rediscovered the ancient city, by chance, fifteen hundred years later, the eruption proved a blessing. For nowhere had the town-planning, daily life, and artistic treasures of the Roman empire been better preserved for posterity than here, where the city had been covered by between thirty and sixty feet of detritus. Pompeii, in the Bay of Naples, was taken totally unaware by the eruption and was preserved by nine feet of ash and mud that kept the air and light from degrading the city and its artifacts.

Today, Pompeii's modern layout is still surprising. The city continues to interest scientists and supply museums across the globe with works of art. It is also a tourist site, receiving two million visitors every year. In the background of the north-facing aerial shot shown here, Vesuvius is visible, which at the time of the eruption was much taller and cone-shaped. In the foreground are the theater and the odeon. On the left are the forum and the administrative district.

▶ **With their sidewalks and paved roadways,** Pompeii's streets were not unlike those of a modern town. Pedestrians walked on the raised block-lined walkways visible in the photo. There was also a water-supply system, with fountains every three hundred feet, where residents had access to drinking water.

A great misfortune for the Pompeians; a gift for historians.

▲ **Because it was tied up with a bronze chain,** this dog could not escape during the eruption and was overwhelmed by the mud and volcanic ash.

▶ **This mule's skeleton was discovered** exactly as shown in the bakery where it turned a wheel to grind the wheat. It is thought that it tried to escape through the door, but finally succumbed, like its fellow mules farther back in the room.

▶ **This resident of Pompeii** tried, like many others, to escape the ash and mud by shutting himself in the basement of his house. But the ash and mud flow was so fast that there was no chance of escape. Scholars believe that Pompeii was home to twenty thousand people at the time of the eruption.

▲ **The ancient world was already familiar with advertising.** This pillar, painted on three sides and perfectly preserved by the mud and ash, publicizes the work of tanners, the artisans who treat animal skins and leather. Such scenes, which are valuable historical evidence, are frequent finds in Pompeii.

▼ **Pompeii had many artists.** Paper was unknown in the Roman period; it did not appear in Europe until the twelfth century. Pompeians wrote on scrolls of papyrus with a stylus or pointed pen, as the people in this painting show.

▼ **This famous bronze statue of a dancing faun** (a Roman minor deity with horns and the feet of a goat) was discovered in the rainwater basin in the center of a domestic courtyard. Originally Greek, it dates from the second century BCE.

▲ **These two bronze statues** represent young men bound for a race in the ancient Olympic Games.

The North Pole ice sheet acts as our planet's thermometer. It is one of the main factors in the world's climate, and it is a capital investment that is diminishing every year because of changing weather patterns.

The Total Pole Airship expedition led by French explorer Jean-Louis Etienne in 2007–2008 was a first. Its aim was to calculate the precise thickness of the northern polar ice sheet in order to provide a benchmark against which changes can be assessed in the upcoming years and decades.

Taking off in an airship, the scientific team made a 1,945-mile overflight of the ice sheet at an altitude of just one hundred feet. Onboard they had an extremely accurate instrument, an EM Bird, that could calculate the thickness of the ice sheet. A year before their eventual journey from Longyearbyen in the Spitsbergen archipelago in Norway to Barrow on the north coast of Alaska, the scientists visited the Russian ice station Barneo, just a few dozen miles from the North Pole. There they spent three weeks with four professional divers, testing their measuring equipment both on and beneath the ice sheet in extremely difficult conditions.

▼ **The Russian ice station Barneo,** not far from the North Pole itself, opens for a month every year in spring. It comprises a dozen tents and a landing strip, and acts as a base camp for explorers and scientists.

▲▼ **Surveying the underwater landscape** is essential in order to place the instruments in the best locations. These divers, experts in extreme conditions, will swim down through an area of open water. Vigilance is needed because the ice re-forms very fast. Here, Jean-Louis Etienne watches as a third diver stays at the surface with his hands on the ropes so as to maintain contact with his two colleagues under the ice sheet. If they find themselves in trouble, they can alert the third diver to help them. He needs to be able to dive at a moment's notice if there is an accident.

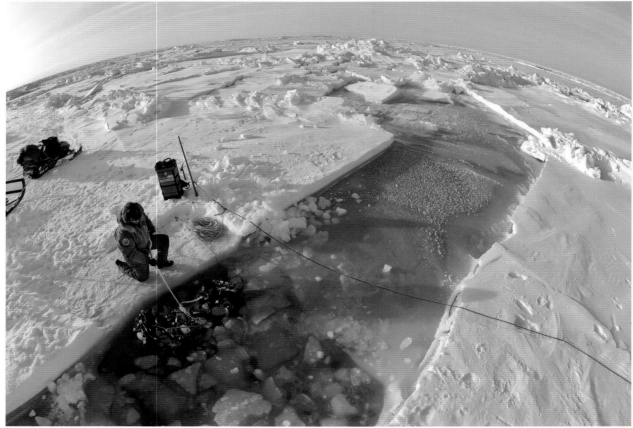

During their second visit under the ice, the divers come face-to-face with some magnificent "ice roses," which have formed because of low temperatures of the ocean's saltwater mixing with the brackish ice of the ice sheet.

Below the ice sheet is a world reminiscent of science fiction.

Divers accompany the ROV (Remote Operating Vehicle) on its first trip under the ice sheet. It measures the shape of the ice with sonar. It emits a sound that helps the ROV measure the distance between the equipment and the ice as it travels back to the ROV. To avoid disturbing the soundings with their air bubbles, the divers will leave the robot to do the remainder of its mission alone.

An unexpected storm at Fayence, in France, grounded the airship and postponed the expedition.

While the airship is pumped up, Jean-Louis Etienne examines the interior, which resembles a cathedral made of cloth.

Before exposure to the harshness of the North Pole, the equipment and the workers had to spend months becoming acclimated. The expedition's six pilots carried out final tests on the airship before flying off toward Paris and Spitsbergen, Norway, the departure base for the trip across the Arctic.

The Baluchitherium

Today, Baluchistan, a province of southern Pakistan, is an arid desert. Thirty million years ago it was a territory covered in luxurious jungle, like the Amazon today. The violent collision of the Indian tectonic plate with the Asian tectonic plate created the Himalayas, bringing about a radical change in climate that caused numerous animals to die out.

After six years' research in an area normally closed to foreigners, a team led by the paleontologist Jean-Loup Welcomme found enough fossils to be able to reconstruct the skeleton of a Baluchitherium, an animal of astonishing dimensions. Comparing the size of the animal's femur (fifty-one inches) to that of a human being (twelve inches), they concluded that they were looking at the largest land-based mammal that had ever lived, nearly twenty feet tall and weighing almost twenty-two tons (i.e., four times the weight of an adult elephant).

To reassemble this enormous skeleton in three dimensions, they had to use more than two hundred fossilized bones originating from different individuals. An idea of this scale is given here by bamboo canes, which measure just over thirty-nine inches each. In the background are the mountains where the bones were found.

The Baluchitherium was an ancestor of the rhinoceros and the largest land-based mammal that ever lived, yet it was an unthreatening herbivore.

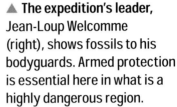

The expedition's leader, Jean-Loup Welcomme (right), shows fossils to his bodyguards. Armed protection is essential here in what is a highly dangerous region.

The small fossils discovered with the bones of the Baluchitherium are an indication of the sorts of plants and animals, shown here, that also existed during the Tertiary period.

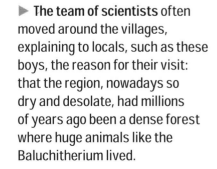

The team of scientists often moved around the villages, explaining to locals, such as these boys, the reason for their visit: that the region, nowadays so dry and desolate, had millions of years ago been a dense forest where huge animals like the Baluchitherium lived.

▲ **Guarded by two Baluchis armed with Kalashnikovs,** the expedition moves around using dromedaries. These animals are the only form of transport that is suited to carrying heavy loads and coping with the rocky landscape and arid climate. Here they are carrying food, tents, and scientific equipment for a month's expedition.

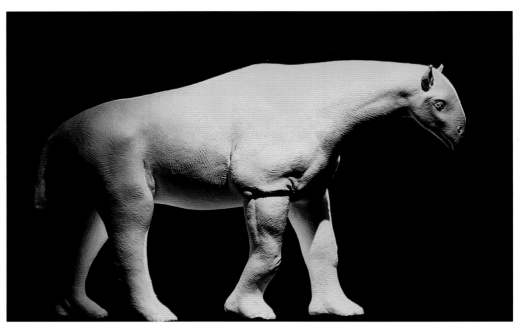

◄ **This three-dimensional reconstruction** of a Baluchitherium was created on a computer from drawings on paper made by the team of scientists.

For almost twelve centuries, ancient Greece dealt with continual warfare between provinces and cities. But every four years there was a miraculous period of peace.

For two whole weeks the citizens of the Greek peninsula's various city-states held a truce in honor of the gods in order to attend games at Olympia, a city of the Peloponnese. A mix of sport, mythology, politics, and artistic endeavor, the ancient Greek games inspired Baron Pierre de Coubertin in 1894 to create the modern Olympic Games with their universal reach and values. The first modern Olympics were played in 1896.

In 2004, the Olympic Games returned to their land of origin. It was an opportunity for a team of well-known trainers, high-achieving sportsmen and sportswomen, and historians to reconstruct at Olympia the locations and demanding sports of the Olympic Games as they had been conducted in ancient times. In those days, training was accompanied by beating drums in a gymnasium (wrestling school) or "palestra." The following pictures depict what the ancient games probably looked like.

▲ **The movements used to throw a discus** were very similar to those made by Olympic competitors today. This reconstruction was filmed by GEDEON Programmes of Paris and involved collaboration by Greek, German, and French historians.

▼ **Chariot racing took place in the hippodrome,** outside of Olympia's sanctuary and stadium. Although athletes competed in very little clothing, chariot drivers wore white tunics.

A unique experiment: a reconstruction of the ancient Olympic Games at Olympia in 2004.

▲ **Of the four races** that were included in the ancient games, the stadion, a single-lap race the length of the stadium, was the shortest and oldest, and therefore the most famous. The winner gave his name to the next Olympiad.

▶ **Winners of events received** a victor's headband and palm branch before taking a lap of honor in the stadium, while the crowd cheered and threw flowers at him. No distinctions were given to competitors who came in second or third place.

Because they were celebrations in honor of the gods of Mount Olympus, the games brought together the best athletes in Greece.

The discus was one of five events that made up the pentathlon (the others being javelin, long jump, running, and wrestling). The perfect positioning of the athlete by the sculptor has made this statue one of the most famous works of art surviving from the ancient world.

▼ **In the background of this aerial shot,** over to the left, is the sacred site of Olympia, one of the Seven Wonders of the Ancient World and Greece's most important religious center during ancient times. To the right is the sacred hill of Mount Kronos. In the middle is the stadium, exposed in 1958 by a team of German archaeologists. The stadium's length (630 feet 9 inches) was the customary length of all stadiums in classical antiquity. Spectators sat on the ground, which sloped inward toward the arena. The slopes had enough space to seat up to forty-five thousand spectators.

◀ **This marble statue of Hermes** carrying the infant Dionysus was discovered in the temple to Hera by German archaeologists around 1880. Since then it has become famous, even appearing on postage stamps.

▶ **The goddess Nike** is represented coming down from heaven to crown the winners of the Olympic Games. This Greek sculpture, once a technical triumph, was the first example of wings portrayed so realistically. The wings have since broken off.

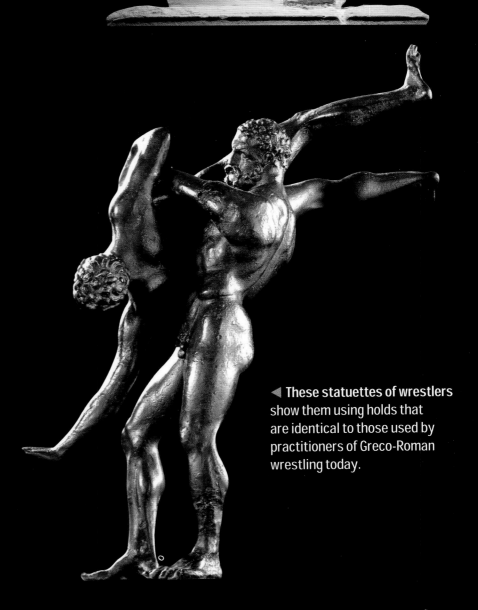

◀ **These statuettes of wrestlers** show them using holds that are identical to those used by practitioners of Greco-Roman wrestling today.

List of Archaeologists

Jean-Yves Empereur

French archaeologist Jean-Yves Empereur is trying to save valuable sites threatened by modern building in the Near East (Greece, Cyprus, Egypt, and Turkey). He has led a large number of excavations both on land and under the sea, most importantly at Alexandria. In 1990, he founded the Center of Alexandrian Studies within the French National Center for Scientific Research (CNRS), and is the current director of the Center for Alexandrian Studies.

Giuseppe Orefici

For the last fifty years, Italian archaeologist Giuseppe Orefici has been tracking down lost civilizations in Latin America. He has directed excavations in Mexico, Nicaragua, Guatemala, Ecuador, Brazil, and, most importantly, Peru, where he discovered Cahuachi, the religious heart of the Nazca region. In 1991, he began exploring Easter Island, and subsequently discovered Polynesia's largest ritual center at Ahu Tongariki.

Françoise Dunand

A former professor at the University of Strasbourg, Françoise Dunand is a French historian who, as a member of Cairo's French Institute for Oriental Archaeology, researches ancient Egyptian religion and civilization. For more than twenty years she has worked on the necropolises of the Kharga Oasis in Egypt, where she leads a team of archaeologists and anthropologists.

Jean-Louis Heim

Son of a botanist committed to the protection of the natural world, the French paleontologist Jean-Louis Heim has been passionate about science since he was a child. His work with the French National Center for Scientific Research (CNRS) has led him to discoveries of the Neanderthals in the Dordogne. He also teaches at the National Museum of Natural History and the Institute of Human Paleontology in Paris.

Roy Chapman Andrews

The American explorer, adventurer, paleontologist, and naturalist Roy Chapman Andrews was born in 1884 and died in 1960, having explored the Gobi Desert and discovered dozens of dinosaur species. Many of his exploits were extremely dangerous—so much so that he is rumored to have been the inspiration for Indiana Jones.

Vassil Dobrev

French archaeologist Vassil Dobrev is a passionate investigator of ancient Egypt and a member of Cairo's French Institute for Oriental Archaeology. He discovered the necropolis of Tabbet al-Guesh in Saqqara, and he is hopeful that his team will eventually find a solution to the mystery of Pharaoh Userkare.

Michel Brunet

French paleoanthropologist and specialist in mammal evolution Michel Brunet discovered the earliest Australopithecus west of the East African Great Rift Valley. Named "Abel," these remains are 3.5 million years old. Brunet also discovered the oldest hominid, Toumaï, some 7 million years old. A recipient of two French state honors—knighthood of the Legion of Honor and membership of the Order of Merit—Brunet is a professor at the prestigious Collège de France in Paris.